27

W

INTERIM SITE

)2

AIR AND FLIGHT

Neil Ardley

Series consultant : Professor Eric Laithwaite

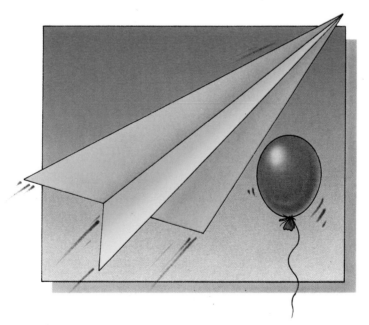

Franklin Watts

London New York Toronto Sydney

The author
Neil Ardley gained a degree in science and worked as
a research chemist and patent agent before entering
publishing. He is now a full-time writer and is the
author of more than fifty information books on
science, natural history and music.

The consultant
Eric Laithwaite is Professor of Heavy Electrical
Engineering at Imperial College, London. A well-
known television personality and broadcaster, he is
best known for his inventions on linear motors.

© 1984 Franklin Watts Ltd

First published in Great
Britain in 1984 by
Franklin Watts Ltd
12a Golden Square
London W1

First published in the United
States of America by
Franklin Watts Inc.
387 Park Avenue South
New York
N.Y. 10016

Printed in Belgium

UK edition:
ISBN 0 86313 158 1
US edition:
ISBN 0-531-03775-4
Library of Congress
Catalog Card Number:
83-51441

Designed by
David Jefferis

Illustrated by Janos Marffy,
Hayward Art Group and
Arthur Tims

AIR AND FLIGHT

Contents

Equipment

In addition to a few everyday items, you will need the following equipment to carry out the activities in this book,

Aluminum cooking foil	Large egg
Apples (2)	Modeling clay
Balloons	Ping-pong ball
Bicycle pump	Potato
Candles	Sink plunger
Detergent	Smooth flat board
Empty plastic bottle	Straws
(with top)	Taper
Funnel	Tumbler
Green plants	Vacuum cleaner (capable
Inner tube	of blowing)

Introduction

Nothing is closer to us than air. It surrounds us all the time and even lies next to our skin under our clothes. Yet we are hardly aware of air. The only time it really makes itself felt is when we have to battle against a strong wind.

Air is nevertheless very important to us. It keeps every living thing alive—even fishes and other water creatures, which breathe oxygen that gets into water from the air. The weather is affected by the way the air in the atmosphere behaves. We put the force that air can exert to use in machines, and we apply the strange effects of moving air to produce flight.

The activities in this book explore the various ways in which air behaves and the ways in which we can use air to make things fly. They include some amazing experiments, such as causing a ball to hover in mid-air and spearing a potato with a straw. Several activities involve matches and candles. Remember to blow them out.

✳ This symbol appears throughout the book. It shows you where to find the scientific explanation for the results of an experiment.

Air is there

Show that air exists and can affect things, even though it is invisible.

△ Take care not to hit the ruler too hard or you may break it.

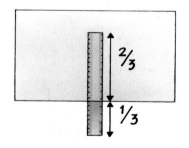

Paper power

Place a ruler on a table so that about one third of its length lies over the edge. Spread a large sheet of paper flat over the ruler as shown. Now strike the end of the ruler to make it fall from the table. The paper holds the ruler down so firmly that it can hardly move.

✴ The air presses down on the sheet of paper. Because the paper is large, the amount of force on it is great. The downward force of the air pressure is enough to stop the end of the ruler beneath the paper moving upward.

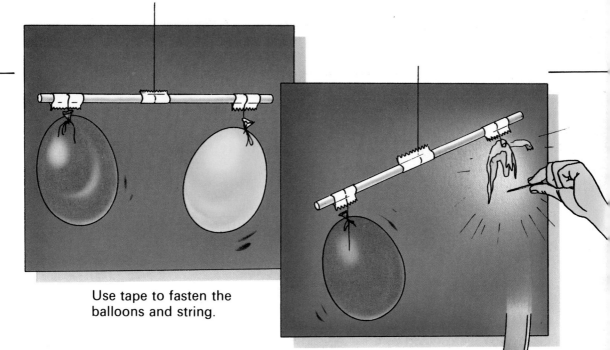

Use tape to fasten the
balloons and string.

Balloon balance

Blow up two large balloons and fasten
them firmly to the ends of a rod about
12 in (30 cm) long, Suspend the rod so that
the balloons balance. Burst one with a
needle. The rod tips. Gather up any pieces
of balloon and attach them to a paper clip.
Fix the clip to the rod in the same place as
the burst balloon. The rod now balances (or
nearly balances) again.

✳ The two balloons balance because the
air inside them has weight. When one
balloon bursts, its air is lost and it loses
weight. The rod tips, just as a seesaw does
if you get off one end. The rod balances
again when you add the pieces of balloon
and paper clip because the paper clip has
about the same weight as the lost air.

△ The rod will tip if
the balloon bursts into
pieces. Replacing the
bits of balloon with a
paper clip shows that
the weight of air in the
balloon makes the rod
balance.

7

What is air?

Investigate the different gases in air.
Find out where one comes from.

Gas burner

Stick a candle to the base of a glass dish.
Fill the dish with water and light the
candle. Place a jar over the candle so that it
rests on some coins just under the surface.
The flame soon goes out and water rises
into the jar.

As the candle burns, it uses up oxygen,
which is one of two main gases in air. As
oxygen is removed from the air inside the
jar, the pressure of the air outside pushes
water up into the jar to take its place.

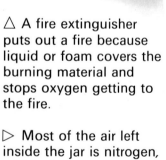

△ A fire extinguisher
puts out a fire because
liquid or foam covers the
burning material and
stops oxygen getting to
the fire.

▷ Most of the air left
inside the jar is nitrogen,
which does not let things
burn.

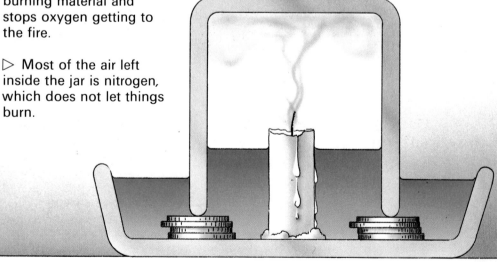

Color the water first by adding a drop of ink and stirring.

Life-giving plants

Collect some green plants—mint is a good choice. Wash and clean the plants under the cold tap, and fill a deep glass bowl with water. Up-end a glass tumbler in the bowl so that it is filled with water. Then put the plants under the rim of the tumbler and place the bowl in the Sun or shine a bright light on it. Bubbles of gas rise from the green plants and collect in the tumbler.

✸ The gas is oxygen, which is made by green plants both on land and in water. The plants use light to make oxygen by a process called photosynthesis. All living things take oxygen from the air to stay alive, and the oxygen gets into the air from plants.

△ All green plants make oxygen like this. Normally you cannot see it happening because the oxygen is invisible and mixes with the air around the plants.

Expanding air

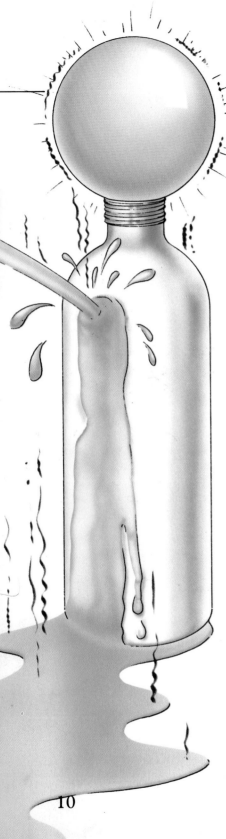

See how air behaves when it gets warmer or colder.

Make a loop of stiff wire and dip it into some detergent.

Lower the wire gently over the neck of the bottle.

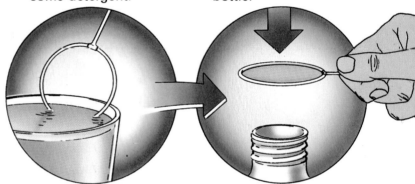

Bubble in a bottle

Take a large bottle and seal the neck with a film of detergent as shown. Place the bottle in the sink and run hot water over it. A bubble grows out of the neck of the bottle. Repeat the experiment using cold water. This time the bubble descends into the bottle.

When hot water is run over the bottle, the air inside gets warmer. This makes it expand in size. The air flows out of the bottle, making the bubble grow larger. When cold water is used, the air in the bottle contracts or gets smaller in size.

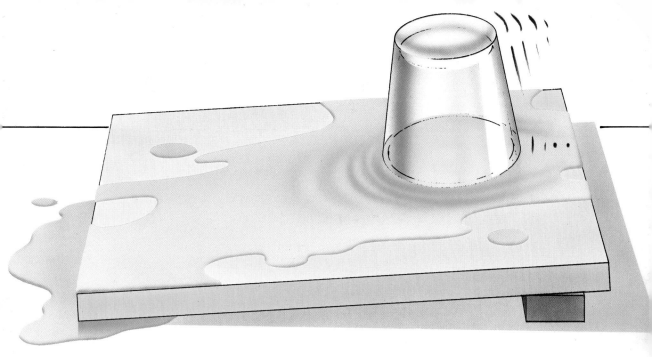

Gliding glasses

Take a smooth, flat board and place an object under one end to make it slope. Wet a glass with cold water and place it upside down on the board. If the glass moves, lower the board until it stops. Now warm the glass under the hot tap. Place it upside down on the board and it glides down!

✳ When the glass is warm, the air inside is heated and it expands. This causes the glass to lift slightly so that it has less grip on the board and slides. You may be able to see bubbles of air coming from the rim.

△ Glasses sometimes move mysteriously down draining boards for this reason.

▽ The jet engines in an aircraft suck in air and heat it. The air then expands and forces the aircraft forward.

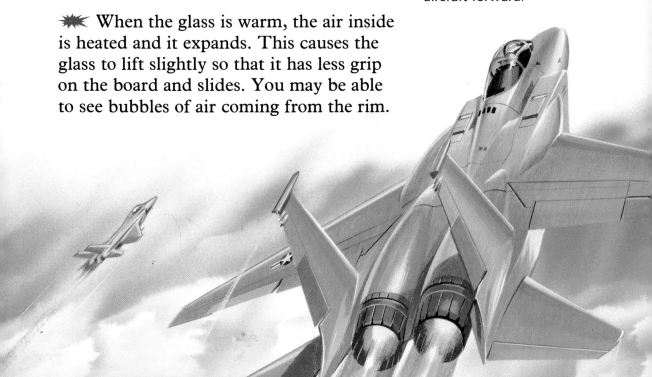

The pressure of air

▽ The hotter and then colder you can make the bottle, the more it collapses. This is because the pressure of air inside the bottle is lowered more if it is cooled more. The pressure of the air outside stays the same.

Demonstrate the strength of the air around you.

Collapsing bottle

Take the top off an empty plastic bottle. Fill the bottle with hot water and empty it. Then put the top back on quickly but firmly, and place the bottle under the cold tap. The sides begin to collapse together as if crushed by a giant invisible hand!

✳ When the bottle is sealed, the air inside is warm. Cooling the bottle lowers the pressure of the air inside. The pressure of the air outside is now higher, so the air surrounding the bottle pushes the sides in until the pressure of the air inside is the same as the pressure outside.

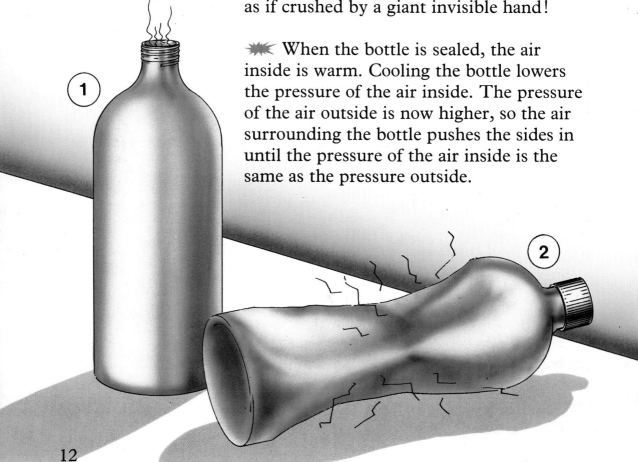

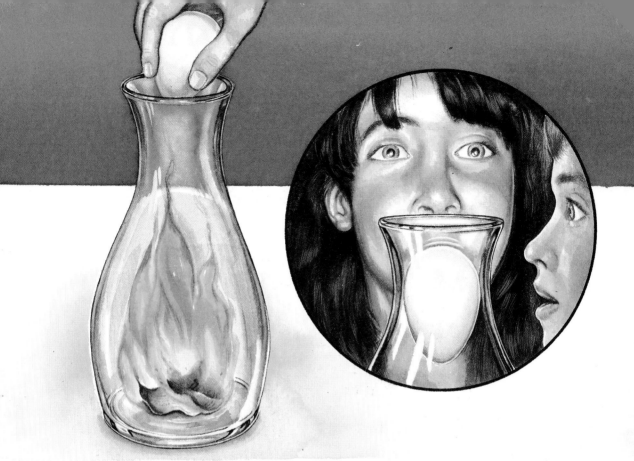

Egg gobbler

Find an egg and a bottle with a neck that is just slightly smaller than the egg. Hard boil the egg by boiling it for six minutes. Cool it and take the shell off. Screw up some paper, drop it into the bottle and light the paper with a taper. Quickly place the egg in the neck of the bottle and it is sucked in, maybe with a pop!

△ To get the egg out again, hold the bottle upside down and shake it until the egg jams in the neck. Then hold the bottle under the hot tap to make the air inside expand and force the egg out.

The burning paper uses up some of the oxygen in the air in the bottle (see page 8). When the egg seals the neck, the pressure of the air inside the bottle falls rapidly as the oxygen is consumed. The air pressure outside pushes the egg in.

13

Air seals

The pressure of the air is strong enough to produce a very tight seal.

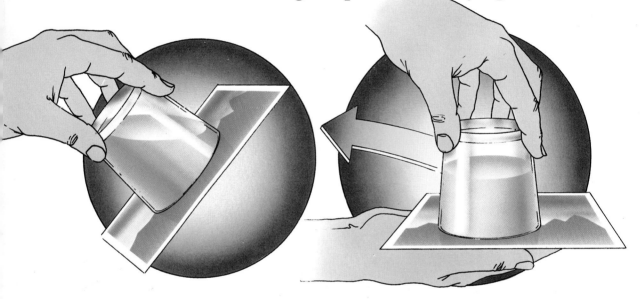

△ To get a good seal, the card must be flat and the rim of the glass must not be chipped. You can then hold the glass at any angle and the water does not fall out. However, try this experiment out over the sink first!

Magic glass

Pour some water in a glass, then lay a picture postcard over the glass with the shiny side down. Hold the card firmly in place and turn the glass upside down. Now take your hand away from the card. The water does not fall out of the glass!

✻ The picture postcard is pressed strongly against the rim of the glass by the pressure of the air outside. The force of this pressure is greater than the weight of water in the glass, so the card supports the water.

14

Plunger power

Take a sink plunger and a small table or a similar object with a flat surface. Press the rubber bowl of the plunger hard against the surface, then lift the handle. The plunger raises the table from the ground!

✸ The bowl bends as you push it against the surface, forcing out air from inside. The rim is pressed flat, so air cannot re-enter the bowl. The bowl then partly regains its shape, making the pressure of the air inside less than the air pressure outside. The air around the bowl therefore forces it hard against the surface, producing a strong seal.

△ To release the plunger, pinch the sides of the bowl between your fingers. This increases the air pressure inside and lifts the rim from the surface so that air can enter the bowl. Now the pressure of air inside is equal to that of the air outside. Rubber suction pads work in the same way as plungers.

Lifting liquids

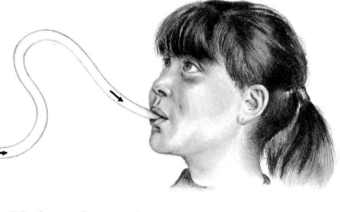

We can make use of air to force water or other liquids up pipes.

Make a fountain

Take a jar with a plastic lid. Make two holes in the lid and seal two straws in it as shown. Replace the lid, and attach a plastic tube to one straw. Hold the jar upside down with the other straw in a bowl of water. Place the tube in your mouth and suck hard. A fountain rises in the jar.

✳ When you suck some air out of the jar the air pressure inside the jar is lowered. The air outside pushes on the water with a greater pressure and forces the water up the straw into the jar. Some mechanical pumps raise water by making the air push water up a pipe in this way.

△ The jar, straws and tube must be airtight. Use modeling clay to seal the straws and lid. You can use two or more straws to raise water from the bowl. Fix the straws together by pinching the end of one and pushing it into the other.

16

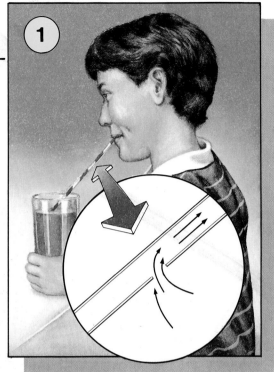

Champion drinker

Without anyone seeing you, pierce a straw with a pin about 1 in (2 cm) from either end. Then give the straw to a friend and challenge him or her to see which of you can suck up a drink fastest. They will take a long time but you can use the same straw to suck it up quickly. Make sure that the lower pinhole is in the drink, and cover the pinhole near your mouth with a finger.

⬥ When you drink with a straw, you lower the air pressure inside your mouth. The air around the liquid forces it up the straw. But if air enters a hole in the straw, the pressure is not lowered as much.

△ Some liquid will be sucked up through the straw with a hole in the air. But it turns into a froth when it meets the air coming through the hole.

The power of air

Increasing the pressure of air can give it enormous power.

△ The straw should go right into the potato so that you can lift it up by the straw.

▽ Pneumatic drills are powered by compressed air. The power of the air forces the blade of the drill down into the road.

Straw spear

Take some straws and a potato. Challenge your friends to prove that they are so strong they can spear the potato with a straw. They will probably fail but you can do it every time. Hold a straw about $2\frac{1}{2}$ in (4 cm) from one end. Squeeze it tightly and plunge this end into the potato very hard.

✺ By squeezing the straw, the air inside cannot escape as it strikes the potato. As the straw goes into the potato, the air space inside gets smaller. This compresses the air (increases its pressure), making the straw firmer so that it pierces the potato and does not bend.

Air support

Lay a deflated inner tube from a bicycle wheel on the ground and cover it with a piece of board. Get someone to sit on the board. Then attach a bicycle pump to the valve of the tube and pump up the tube. The board begins to rise into the air, even though someone is sitting on it.

⬖ As you keep pumping air into the tube, the air pressure inside increases. It exerts more and more force on the tube, making it expand in size. When this force is greater than the weight of the board and person, the air in the tube lifts the board.

△ The air in a tire is compressed so much that the high pressure produces enough force to support the vehicle. In a car tire, the air pressure is about twice the pressure of the outside air.

▽ Stop pumping when the board lifts, or you may burst the tube!

19

Moving air

Air flowing around objects may cause them to behave in unexpected ways.

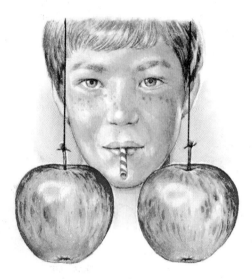

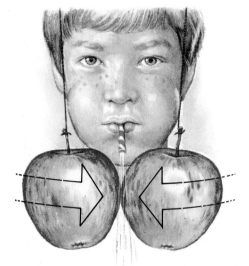

△ You can use any pair of medium-sized objects instead of apples, provided they both have curved surfaces.

Blown together

Suspend two apples so that they are about $\frac{1}{2}$ in (1 cm) apart. Stop them swinging. Then take a straw and blow a stream of air between the apples. Instead of being blown apart, they are first pulled together!

⁂ As the air flows between the apples, it is deflected by the curved surface of each apple and it speeds up. Fast-moving air has a lower pressure than still or slow-moving air. The air pressure on the outside of each apple is now greater. It pushes both apples into the stream of air.

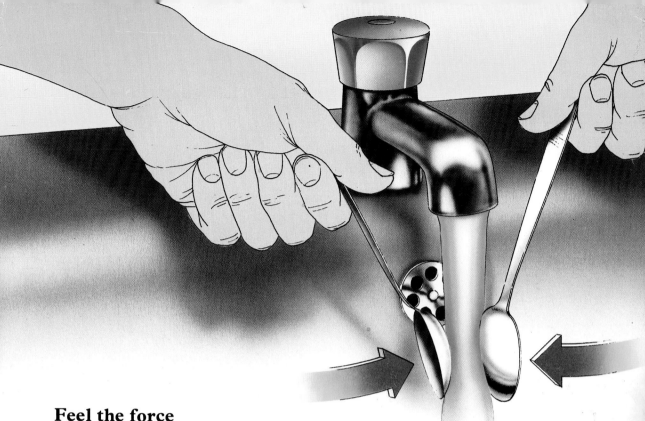

Feel the force

Turn on a tap and hold two spoons loosely between the fingers of each hand. Bring the spoons up to the stream of water as shown. As soon as the water flows over the backs of the spoons, it pulls the spoons together. Now move the handles away from each other. The spoons still cling together, even though they are being pulled apart.

※ This experiment is similar to the last one. But this time water is used instead of air, so that you can easily feel the force pulling the objects together. This happens because the water flows faster over the curved backs of the spoons and its pressure is lowered. The air pressure outside the stream is stronger, and pushes the two spoons together.

▽ The top surface of the wing of an aircraft or bird is curved like the back of a spoon. Air flowing over and under a wing produces a force that lifts the wing, just as the spoon is pulled into the moving stream of water.

Continued overleaf

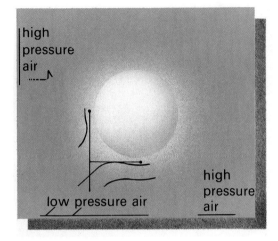

pressure
air

high
pressure
air

low pressure air

Hoverball

Make a vacuum cleaner blow air out instead of sucking it in. Point the pipe up into the air and place a ping-pong ball over it. Let go, and the ball rises to hover in mid-air above the pipe. Tilt the pipe and the ball floats away as if suspended by an invisible thread!

△ Try adding a second or third ball. See how placing your hand in the airstream affects it.

✳ The stream of air flows faster around the curved sides of the ball. The air pressure here is lowered, and the higher air pressure outside the airstream pushes the ball into the middle of the airstream. This force, the push of the air against the ball and the weight of the ball all combine to make it hover in mid-air.

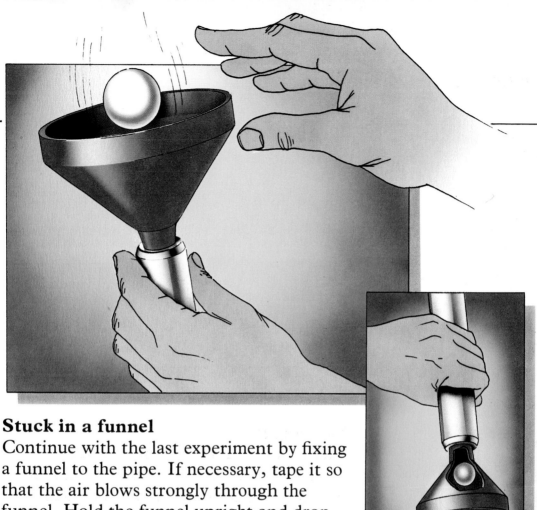

Stuck in a funnel

Continue with the last experiment by fixing a funnel to the pipe. If necessary, tape it so that the air blows strongly through the funnel. Hold the funnel upright and drop the ping-pong ball into it. The ball is sucked down, not blown out! Now turn the funnel upside down. The ball is held in the funnel and does not fall out.

☀ As the air comes out into the funnel, it flows fast around the curved surface of the ball. The air pressure there is lowered, and the greater air pressure in the rest of the funnel pushes the ball into the funnel. This force is strong enough to overcome both the ball's weight and the force of the air that tries to push the ball out.

△ If you can blow hard enough and for long enough, you can do this experiment by blowing into the funnel with your mouth.

23

Wings for flight

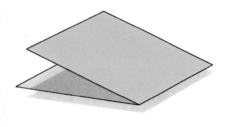

△ Make the wing with a flat sheet of paper measuring about 8 in (20 cm) by 12 in (30 cm). Fold it in two across and tape the top half to the bottom half so that the edges are about ½ in (1 cm) apart. You may be able to make the wing rise by blowing with your mouth.

See how wings work and construct a simple, winged aircraft.

Paper wing

Construct a wing from a sheet of paper as shown. Slip a long rod or ruler through the wing, and direct a stream of air at it using a vacuum cleaner (see page 22). The wing rises as air blows over the wing, but when it stops, the wing falls back.

✳ As the air flows over the curved upper surface of the wing, it moves faster and its pressure falls. The greater pressure of the slower air underneath the wing pushes the wing up into the air. The same thing happens when the wings of a bird or aircraft move through the air, and this is why they can fly.

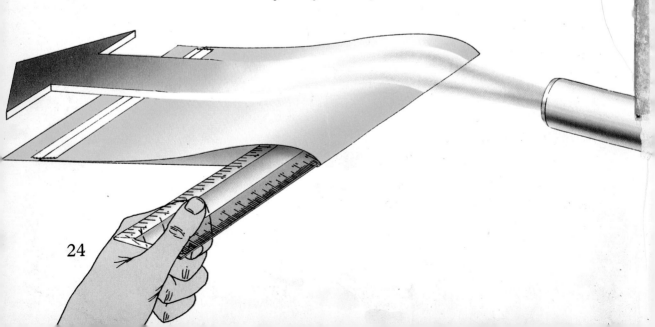

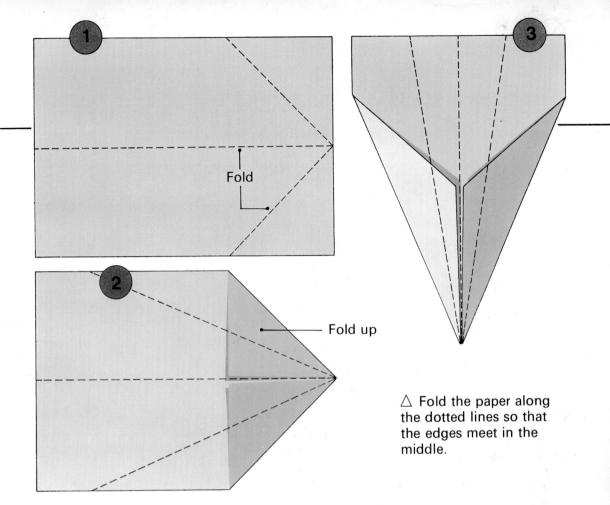

1

Fold

2

Fold up

3

△ Fold the paper along the dotted lines so that the edges meet in the middle.

Dart glider

Make a paper dart as shown. The dart will glide well if you curve the top surfaces of the wings. Make flaps (called ailerons) by folding the back edges of the wings up or down. The dart will roll if one aileron is up and the other is down.

✳ Curving the top surfaces of the wings helps to lift the dart so that it stays up in the air. The ailerons also affect the flow of air over the dart and change its flight. Aircraft have ailerons and other flaps to assist in take off, turning and landing.

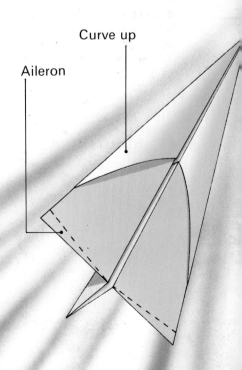

Curve up

Aileron

Up into the air

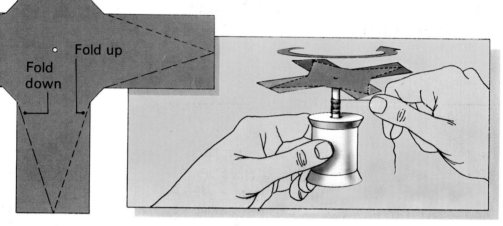

Helicopters and balloons can fly too—and without any wings.

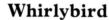
Fold up
Fold down

△ Try making rotors of different shapes to see how they work. You may be able to get the rotor to fly up and out of the reel.

Whirlybird

Cut a cross from a piece of card and twist the arms to make a rotor. Firmly fix a short rod to the card. It must be narrow enough to go through a wooden spool. Next wind a length of strong thin thread around the rod just beneath the rotor. Place the rod in the spool and pull the thread. The rotor spins, lifting the rod up into the air.

As the rotor spins, it blows air down like a ceiling fan. This action lifts the rotor and rod. The whirling blades of the rotor of a helicopter lift it into the air in the same way. The rotor can be tilted to make the helicopter fly forward or backward.

Hot-air seesaw

Make two large cups of aluminum cooking foil and fasten the cups upside down to each end of a rod. Suspend the rod so that the two cups balance. Put some lighted candles under one of the cups. The cup rises, tipping the balance. Take away the candle and the cup descends, like a seesaw.

✳ Air heated by the candle expands. This makes the hot air lighter than the surrounding cool air, so it rises. The warm air flows into the foil cup, making it lighter also, and so it rises. When the air inside cools, the cup descends.

Warning: Take care not to burn yourself.

△ Hot-air balloons make use of heated air to lift them into the sky. To descend, the air is allowed to cool so that it loses its lifting power.

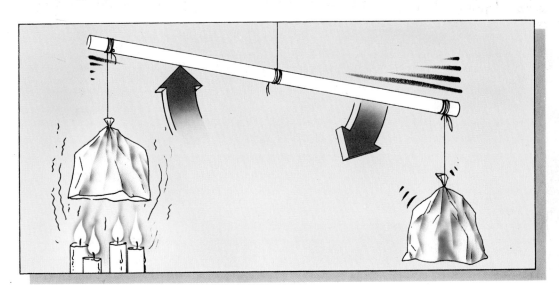

Measuring the air

△ Weather people use anemometers to measure wind speeds. This instrument has three cups that spin around in the wind.

▽ Draw a scale to show wind speeds, and set the indicator so that it shows zero out of the wind.

Make two instruments for comparing the speed and pressure of air.

Wind speed indicator
Insert a large screw in a piece of wood. Then wind some wire around the handle of a plastic spoon and hang it from the screw as shown. Face the bowl of the spoon in the direction of the wind, and it will swing by an amount depending on the wind speed.

The wind pushes more strongly on the bowl of the spoon as it blows faster. The spoon swings until its weight stops it moving any farther. The angle by which it swings indicates the speed of the wind.

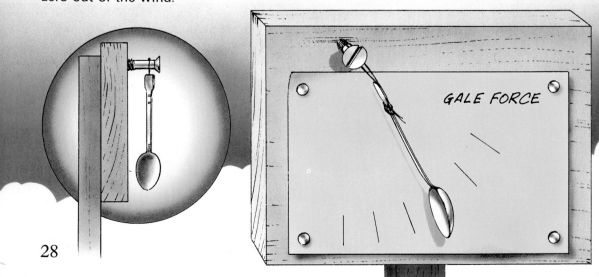

GALE FORCE

Basic barometer

Take a glass jar with a wide top. Cut a piece of rubber from a balloon and stretch it tightly across the top. Then tape a long pointer, such as a straw, to the rubber as shown. Put this barometer out of the way and place a card beside the pointer. Mark its position on different days and see how it moves up and down.

✳ The barometer pointer indicates how the pressure of the air changes — up for high, down for low. This is because the air inside the jar expands or contracts as the air pressure outside decreases or increases. The expansion or contraction makes the rubber cover move up and down, and so the pointer moves too.

△ The temperature of the air also affects this barometer. Use a thermometer to check that the temperature is the same when using it.

▽ Pressure changes affect the weather, so weather maps have lines that indicate the air pressure at different places.

More about air and flight

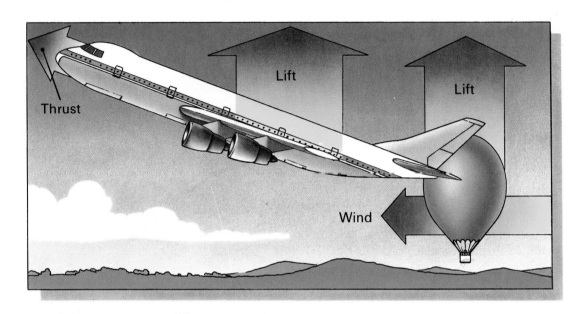

Thrust

Lift

Lift

Wind

Air

Air is a mixture of gases. It contains 21% oxygen, 78% nitrogen and 1% argon. There are also very small amounts of carbon dioxide and rare gases, which include neon and helium. The proportions of these gases in the air are the same throughout the world. But in any place the air may also contain water vapor and dust, as well as polluting gases from factories and vehicles. The amounts vary from place to place.

Air pressure

The pressure of the air around us is caused by the weight of all the air above our heads pressing down on everything on the ground. It is equal to a weight of about 1 kg placed on every sq cm of a surface (about 15 lb on every sq in). We do not normally feel this pressure because the air inside our bodies is at the same pressure.

We can increase the pressure of air inside a container, for example, by heating it or pumping

△ The thrust (power) of an aircraft's engines pushes it forward. At the same time, the movement of the wings through the air produces lift (a lifting force) that carries it up. A balloon also has lift but the wind pushes it forward through the air.

air into it. If the container can expand, like a balloon, the increase in pressure will make it get bigger. If we lower the pressure, the container will get smaller if possible.

30

Atmosphere

The atmosphere is the layer of air that surrounds the Earth. We live at the bottom of the atmosphere, which is about 160 km deep (100 miles).

Barometer

A barometer is an instrument for measuring the pressure of the air in the atmosphere. It is used in weather forecasting because changes in pressure can help to tell what the weather will be like.

Flight

To fly, winged aircraft and birds have to move forward as they lift themselves up into the air. To move, powered aircraft use engines. Birds flap their wings to push themselves forward. A glider or a soaring bird normally points slightly downward so that its weight carries it forward. The movement of the wings through the air provides lift, but a glider or soaring bird may gain height by flying into

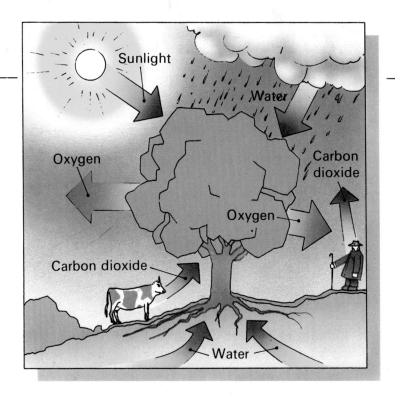

rising air currents.

The whirling blades of a helicopter work as moving wings to raise it into the air. The blades also work like a propeller to push the helicopter forward. Balloons contain light gases or hot air to lift them into the sky. The wind moves a balloon forward.

Photosynthesis

Green plants take in carbon dioxide from the air or water and also water or water vapor.

They use the energy in sunlight to change the carbon dioxide and

△ Trees and other green plants take in carbon dioxide breathed out by animals and people and also water. They then turn them into oxygen and plant food by photosynthesis.

water into oxygen and plant foods. This is how plants stay alive.

Animals and people live by breathing in oxygen from the air. They breathe out carbon dioxide. Green plants take it in and use it to make oxygen again. In this way, the amount of oxygen in the air stays the same.

31

Index

PRINTED IN BELGIUM BY
proost
INTERNATIONAL BOOK PRODUCTION